D0429554

THE GARDEN
TRELLIS

THE LIBRARY *of* GARDEN DETAIL

THE GARDEN
TRELLIS

ROY STRONG

Simon and Schuster

New York   London   Toronto   Sydney   Tokyo   Singapore

Simon and Schuster

Simon & Schuster Building

Rockefeller Center

1230 Avenue of the Americas

New York, New York 10020

First published in Great Britain in 1991 by
Pavilion Books Limited
196 Shaftesbury Avenue, London WC2H 8JL

Designed by Paul Burcher
Printed and bound in Italy by L.E.G.O., Vicenza

Library of Congress Cataloguing in Publication Data

Strong, Roy C.
    The garden trellis/Roy Strong.
        p. cm.—(The Library of garden detail)
    "First published in Great Britain in 1991 by Pavilion Books
    Limited"—T.p. verso.
        ISBN 0-671-74404-6
        1. Trellises. I. Title. II. Series.
    SB473.5.S76 1991
    717—dc20
                                                91-9644
                                                CIP

        10   9   8   7   6   5   4   3   2   1

CONTENTS

❦

INTRODUCTION
page 7

STRUCTURE
page 25

FRAMING DEVICES
page 34

PLANT SUPPORT
page 45

PURE ORNAMENT
page 54

SOURCES
page 62

CREDITS
page 63

6

J N T R O D U C T I O N

RELLIS IS ONE OF THE GREAT AND FORGOTTEN ELEMENTS in garden-making. At first made of willow or nut-pole and later of Spanish chestnut, for centuries it contributed to those masterpieces of the carpenter's art that enriched the gardens of the palaces and country houses of the renaissance and baroque ages. We can see this today, for example, in the re-created renaissance garden at Villandry in France, where the *potager* beds are contained within rectangular enclosures and arbours of trelliswork. For the renaissance man, trelliswork had a deep attraction, for it distilled his fascination for the complex interplay between the twin worlds of art and nature whose arena was the garden. Trees and plants were trained against trellis with the intention of merging art and nature into something which was neither wholly one or the other.

The renaissance use of trellis exceeded anything attempted in our own age, reflecting the passion for private hideaways, rooms in which trelliswork and plant life were welded into quasi-architectural constructions of the utmost fantasy. At the same time it was utilized in the humblest manner, as a support for espaliered fruit trees along garden walls. The great gardens of the Italian renaissance were famous for their trelliswork – of which not a stick now remains; we should remember this when visiting surviving gardens today – though their full splendour can only be evoked by contemporary pictures and engravings.

In the seventeenth century it was the Dutch who became famed for their skills in trelliswork or, as it was more widely known in French, *treillage*. The great French gardener, André le Nôtre, creator of Versailles for Louis XIV, employed Dutch craftsmen for the trellis porticos and pavilions at Chantilly in the 1670s: '*Les Hollandais sont les plus habiles gens du monde pour toutes sortes de cabinets.*' This Netherlandish skill is caught in a famous pattern-book

1. Treillage *of the golden age re-created at Het Loo in The Netherlands. This magnificent construction epitomizes the essence of the art.*

which first appeared in 1669 and went through many editions into the eighteenth century, Jan van der Groen's *Den Nedelandtsen Hovenier* (The Dutch Gardener). Its pages of designs for buildings, arches, tunnels, vases and garden seats remain an inspiration to us today.

By the seventeenth century *treillage* had developed into a highly sophisticated garden art in its own right. Trellis

*2. Trellis arcading dappled with vine leaves in sunset autumn colours.
Whole galleries and corridors may be constructed of trellis.*

pyramids and obelisks were used as focal points to the
elaborate parterres. Garden vistas would be terminated by
classical architecture in trellis. Tunnel arbours, inherited
from the Middle Ages, were also made of trellis and
remained in fashion until the close of the century. In the
re-created baroque garden of William III at Het Loo in The
Netherlands, we can see such an arbour replete with
galleries, domed rooms and windows looking out on to a

parterre. Painted blue-green it has hornbeam trained over it to create a leafy corridor. A corridor of another kind was often made by training trees at a distance from a wall and then entwining their branches through trellis to form a roof.

At its height, Versailles utilized vast stretches of trellis – in the main of wood but sometimes of iron (metal was much used with wood at the end of the seventeenth and beginning of the eighteenth centuries, but most extant metal *treillage* is Victorian). From 1674 onwards trellis covered with some climbing plant, jasmine, honeysuckle or roses, replaced hedges to etch in the *allées* in the *bosquets*. Here the trellis was of sweet chestnut and painted green. Today we can see that effect being re-created, a beautiful one waiting to be copied as a means of articulating inexpensively the shrubberies of our own time.

This trellis art gradually spread through Western Europe into Russia and across the Atlantic to the New World. The restored boxwood gardens of Virginia, such as Gunston Hall for example, contain elegant examples of the

11

art, all the more appealing to us today on account of their modesty and simplicity.

Inevitably this golden age of trellis was doomed when the landscape style took over, first in England and then as *le jardin anglais* in the rest of Europe. It was not until the revival of the formal garden at the opening of the nineteenth century that there was a conscious return to the use of trellis as architecture. The person responsible for that revival was the landscape architect, Humphry Repton, who made extensive use of trellis from arches for flower gardens to verandahs for country cottages. The garden designer Harold Peto also made use of it for Daisy, Countess of Warwick, in the romantic revivalist garden he designed for her at Easton Lodge in 1902 in response to Francis Bacon's 'covered alley upon carpenter's work', although Peto's inspiration was to be the *treillage* of sixteenth-century France.

This vigorous but short-lived revival lasted in England until 1914 and World War I brought the collapse of country house culture. The rose garden was the *treillage*

3. *A* treillage *rose pergola in the sumptuous manner of the* Belle
Epoque. *Although a triumph, the problems of repairing and replacing
such a structure should always be borne in mind when erecting it.*

paradise. Whole rose gardens were constructed from trellis: walls, arches, arbours, trainers, fans, pyramids, temples and pillars. Trellis offered support for virtually every form of rambler, climber and pillar rose. A catalogue of what was

4. *A fine example of an inexpensive garden pavilion made from ordinary trellis designed to be engulfed by roses.*

available c.1910 from the Pyghtle Works at Bedford is a revelation. There are no less than sixteen different types of trellis fencing, twelve types of arch, four varieties of arbour besides three forms of rose temple. 'These', the catalogue informs its readers, 'will be found exceedingly pretty and useful when covered with climbing roses or, in fact, any creeper where the trees are newly planted and do not afford shade; and their moderate cost brings them within reach of everyone?' What a mighty tradition we have lost!

So what of today? Trellis exists, of course, but on the whole lacks the imagination that made it once a glory in the garden. It can still be purchased in its most rudimentary form at the humblest of garden suppliers, usually concertina-ed to open up into a pattern of diamond-paned lattice. But racks of trelliswork panels are also available in various sizes, and specialist manufacturers can provide excellent trellis panels in different meshes and thicknesses, and with different colour finishes and period flourishes such as a gothic cornicing along the top. With these we move into more exciting possibilities – those of creating architectural structures: walls, enclosures and supports, arches and sections which can, with careful planning, be used to create major features for your garden at minimum cost.

Treillage is the French for sturdy trellis but is frequently also used to mean the art of using trellis. Spectacular effects can be achieved to lift the dullest of enclosures. There is only one drawback: trellis is ephemeral, with a life of perhaps twenty years after which major replacements will be called for. On the other hand it is its transitory nature which bestows upon it an almost fairytale quality. It provides the garden with transparent architecture with all the visual paradox that that implies. Walls, temples, columns, obelisks, arches and arbours are there and yet not there.

Sometimes they are transformed into walls of evergreen by climbing plants such as ivy. Sometimes they are garlanded with roses, clematis, honeysuckle, vines and a hundred other climbers, with leaves, flowers and fruit soaring heavenwards so that at times they seem to explode into the sky only to cascade down upon us in pell mell profusion. And in winter the spidery sprawling branches of the climbers make an intriguing counterpoint to the

5. *Trellis always brings with it an intriguing response to the play of light casting patterned shadows around it. In this instance a trellis wall excites the visitor as to what lies beyond.*

angularity of the structure. Trellis structures produce wonderful effects of broken light casting across their surroundings a diaper pattern of shadows which can be most stunning on a crisp sunny winter's day.

Here indeed is an inexpensive way of adding style to any garden. The simplest garden seat is transformed into a beguiling arbour by the addition of a trellis frame – when your trellis should be clothed with sweet-smelling climbers; a honeysuckle and an old-fashioned perfumed rose can rarely be bettered. That perennial problem of a long narrow garden can be solved immediately by running a trellis fence across it, and creating a clairvoyée to give the visitor tantalizing glimpses of what lies beyond.

Every garden needs a focal point. A trellis pavilion at a crossing is an elementary construction, and clothed with climbers would be a handsome one. And what about the vegetable garden? A tunnel of trellis up which you can train runner beans or tomato plants would transform it into a decorative *potager*. A panel of trellis set into a garden gate

6. *Trellis transforming a back garden from a dull wattle-fenced enclosure into a verdant inviting bower. Attached to the top of the fencing it gives privacy and support to climbers. With the skilful addition of a few posts and a roof it has made a minute gazebo.*

20

7. *The modest porch of a country
cottage enlivened by a clematis clambering up
a strip of trellis.*

adds anticipatory mystery. Run larch poles along a path and top them with a ceiling of trellis and you have a pergola up which to train wisteria, roses, a vine or what you will. If you lack privacy run panels of trellis along the top of boundary walls and fences and train evergreens on them. Attach it lower down to the same walls and fences and train fruit trees into patterns. Be bold and experiment. If you are really adventurous you will want to attempt trellis *trompe l'œil*, the art of superimposing trellis architecture on to walls using false perspective.

21

Nowadays we tend either to leave trellis in natural wood impregnated with preservative or paint it white. Why not revive those colours of previous centuries? Green and blue or indeed blue-green are almost unbeatable colours for *treillage*, far more subtle in the world of nature than restless and startling white. I have also seen China red and black used to great effect. Always consider colour choice carefully, both in the context of its location and the plants you intend to train over it.

Trellis will open up the whole world of climbing plants. Always consider whether you wish the trellis to be completely lost or whether you would like some of the plant's support structure to be seen. I would always prefer to see a little at least of the architecture, softened only and not smothered by the plant. Remember that trellis will not last for ever, and take that into account when training a plant up it; you might one day have to replace a section without damaging the plant. Take into account also the time you have available to do garden work. It is no use planting a beautiful rambling rose or wisteria if you have no intention of pruning it!

Aspect is as important when choosing your climbers as it is with any garden plant. You will need to check in particular what will thrive on a cold north facing surface. Where several are required, assemble a combination with contrasting flower colour, leaf shape and varying seasonal habit to provide year-round interest.

Everyone will have their own preference but amongst my

8. *Two rough brick pillars are joined by trellis to form a rose window, with glimpses beyond of trellis fencing containing the garden.*

favourites would be a *Vitis coignetiae* with its sweetly scented flower clusters in summer and amazing sunset foliage in the autumn; an early or late Dutch honeysuckle (*Lonicera periclymenum* 'Belgica' and 'Serotina') would provide heady perfume from pretty flowerheads falling in cascades; the abutilons are good value, fast growing and with an abundance of colourful flowers all through the summer months (*Abutilon megapotamicum* is a wonderfully graceful climber with dark green leaves and showers of exotic orange and yellow flowers).

Roses are inevitable and the range enormous. After well over a century the climber 'Gloire de Dijon' still holds its own with its soft tints of yellow and apricot. 'Pink Perpetué' is lovely too with its clusters of fragrant two-toned pink flowers. Amongst the ramblers 'Alberic Barbier' provides a mass of thick green foliage as a background for small creamy white blooms. And sentiment still binds me to the richly scented salmon pink 'Albertine'. Everyone will have their own favourites and a rose also allows for a clematis scrabbling through it.

Soon both plants and your trellis will be contributing to your garden's beauty. You will be able to measure your success when your visitors admire the flowers but also compliment you on your mastery of the lost art of *treillage* in the garden.

STRUCTURE

9. *A refreshingly contemporary use of a sturdy rectangular trellis for a garden house. The main house also makes unusual use of trellis for its balconies and staircases.*

25

26

10. *In this re-creation of a great French renaissance château garden at Villandry in France, we see the continuation of the medieval practice of enclosing a garden with an ordinary trellis fence. This simple idea could easily be copied today, for example, around a vegetable garden.*

11. *Pyramids of transparent trellis contrast with the solidity of clipped box topiary in this rose garden. Both give year-round garden structure but in summer the pyramids would be clothed with roses.*

12. *An American garden given immediate style by an arbour set into a wall of trellis. The difference in gauge of the two trellises is worth consideration.*

28

13. *Trellis is an extremely effective form of fencing, showing interesting colour contrasts between handsome terracotta pillars with golden finials and the green trellis panels. The effect of tracery is heightened by the sunlight.*

29

14. *Two silver-leaved weeping pears (*Pyrus salicifolia *'Pendula')*
flank a trellis gateway leading to a sundial. Trellis makes instant garden
rooms, and this can often be valuable while waiting for hedges to grow
in the early stages of a garden.

30

15. *A stylish small enclosure making successful use of seemingly disparate elements. Raised beds in the manner of Versailles tubs, and oriental touches in the way of stones and gravel are unified by the small gauge trellis fence.*

16. *A wonderful rooftop container garden in which the use of screens of cheap trellis to support climbers and make tiny rooms contributes much.*

17. *Tiny walled gardens of Victorian terrace houses are perennial problems. This one has been ingeniously lifted by adding trellis above the wall and treating the whole space as a summer living room.*

18. *A small town garden with ambitious effects partly achieved by the use of trellis as walls for the Chinese-style pavilion and for the panels of the bridge. Wisely it has been painted a greeny blue. White or off-white would make this calming verdant enclosure only restless and strident.*

ℱRAMING

𝒟EVICES

34

19. Wintry light seen here looking out through the straight lines of trellis
to the bending branches of trees and bushes beyond.

20. A garden focal point composed of easily available materials: timber infilled with trellis. With a little imagination variants of a structure of this type can be created in almost any garden.

36

21. *Reconstructed seventeenth-century* treillage *on the grand scale in the great baroque garden of William III's palace at Het Loo in The Netherlands. The Dutch were famous for their trelliswork; here the tunnel arbour has hornbeam* (Carpinus betulus) *trained over it.*

22. *A trellis arch leads into a grape tunnel with the leaves turning pale gold in a dramatic play of light on both the vine and its supporting architecture.*

38

23. *A gothic* treillage *arch in one of a pair of facing pavilions, giving a glimpse through a cut in a stilt hornbeam hedge. A golden hop (*Humulus lupulus aureus*) has been trailed through the trellis.*

*24. A dreamlike vista leading to a trellis arbour used as a
canopy for a statue. Once again, stone and wood make a satisfying
alliance in creating a garden tableau.*

25. *A simple trellis arch framing a view along a path in a* jardin potager. *Box-edged borders on either side conceal the vegetable beds behind them. The view is from within.*

26. *This time looking into a trellis pavilion.*
Notice how it has been cleverly used as the
culmination of one garden and the gateway to
another.

42

27. An arbour of carpenter's work and trellis with a vine at the back and
a rose over it. I would prefer the seat just a little less heavy and large.

*28. An American variant on the arbour theme. The wood is stained grey,
pleasantly keeping the markings of the grain.*

44

*29. A simple garden seat completely transformed
by the addition of a trellis arbour over which
white clematis cascades.*

$\mathcal{P}$LANT

$\mathcal{S}$UPPORT

30. *A very fine gauge trellis painted green and making a handsome support for a potted fuschia.*

46

31. *Folding trellis used in a border as a support. Trellis never looks out of place applied in such a way, but avoid painting it white and stick to natural wood or green.*

32. *A simple arbour made of trellis and within the capabilities of any handyman. A golden hop (*Humulus lupulus aureus*) has transformed it into a sylvan bower in which to sit and contemplate.*

33. (right) *A happy contrast of the small-leaved passion flower meandering its way across an ordinary panel of trellis.*

48

34. (above) *A vine will provide a glorious mutation of leaf colour in the autumn, ranging through the yellows and ochres to deep claret and purple. The vine leaf makes a handsome contrast with the angularity of the trellis.*

49

35. *Trellis supporting a honeysuckle which tumbles over and engulfs a door with its heady sweet-smelling fragrance.*

50

36. *The elementary but satisfactory juxtaposition*
of flowering plants – foxgloves, geraniums, a fuschia
and a clematis – with sturdy trellis fencing.

37. *One of the simplest uses of trellis is against a wall, in this instance supporting* Fremontodendron californicum *'California Glory' with its pretty yellow flowers.*

52

38. *Here clay pots containing* Bidens aurea
*enliven a well-placed panel of white trellis. The
panel successfully links the two different windows
making a lively corner.*

39. *The rose garden benefited most from the* treillage *revival at the end of the nineteenth century. Here we see this at its grandest with roses garlanding whole temples of trelliswork. Notice how effective it is as a setting for statuary.*

$\mathcal{P}$URE

$\mathcal{O}$RNAMENT

54

40. *A trellis pavilion for alfresco meals sited beneath the branches*
of a splendid tree in Louisiana. Any serious application of climbers would
only detract from the architectural elegance of this garden building.

41. *Trellis used for a very modest gate.*

56

42. *Romantic elegance of a high order achieved by means of a
combination of clipped evergreens, a rose arch and a white lattice gate.
Again, the contrast between the gauge of the gate and fence trellis adds
to the sense of style.*

43. *A masterpiece of architectural* treillage *transforming what would otherwise be a dull brick wall on a terrace. Notice how the plants are used to soften the effect but also how the architecture is allowed to retain its integrity without being smothered.*

58

44. *These delightful arbours at Villandry, made
by attaching trellis to a stout wooden frame,
would not be difficult to adapt and copy.*

45. *Recent* **trompe l'œil treillage** *in the style of the eighteenth century applied to a wall of an old French château. The recession achieved by false perspective will be heightened when the thuja arch is complete.*

60

46. *A* treillage *pavilion straddles the path in a Louisiana garden,*
offering both protection from the sun and vistas from it.

61

47. *A charming trellis aviary set at the water's edge and ingeniously masquerading as a summer house.*

S O U R C E S

Some UK Addresses	*Some US Addresses*

Some UK Addresses

Ollerton Engineering
Goosefoot Lane
Salmesbury Bottoms
Preston
Lancashire
PR5 0RN
Telephone: (025 485) 2127/4121

Stuart Garden Architecture
Larchfield Estate
Ilminster
Somerset
TA19 0PF
Telephone: (0460) 57862

The Trellis Shop
Outside Inside
68 Fortune Green Road
West Hampstead
London
NW6 1DS
Telephone: (071) 431 5781

Some US Addresses

Dalton Gazebos
7260-68 Oakley St
Philadelphia, PA 19111
Telephone: (215) 342-9804

International Terracotta Inc.
690 North Robertson Boulevard
Los Angeles, CA 90069-5088
Telephone: (213) 657-3752

Moultrie Manufacturing Co.
PO Drawer 1179
Moultrie, GA 31776 1179
Telephone: (800) 841-86741
in Georgia (912) 985-1312

Smith and Hawken
25 Corte Madera
Mill Valley, CA 94941
Telephone: (415) 383 4415

Vintage Gazebos
Dept 367
513 S. Adams
Fredericksburg, TX 78624
Telephone: (513) 997-9513

Walpole Woodworkers
767 East St
Walpole, MA 02081
Telephone: (617) 668-2800

PICTURE CREDITS

The Publisher thanks the following photographers and organizations for their kind permission to reproduce photographs in this book.
Owners and designers of gardens are credited where known.
Photographers appear in bold type.

Title page. **The Garden Picture Library/Gary Rogers**; private garden
page 6. **Marijke Heuff**; Herrenhausen, Germany
Picture No 1 **The Garden Picture Library/Henk Dijkman)**; Het Loo, The Netherlands
Picture No 2 **Marijke Heuff**; Schwetzingen, Germany
Picture No 3 **The Garden Picture Library/Brigitte Thomas**; The National Trust, Bodnant, Gwynedd
Picture No 4 **Marijke Heuff**; Mr & Mrs Lane Fox, Hazelby House, Berkshire
Picture No 5 **Andrew Lawson**; Gothic House, Charlbury, Oxfordshire
Picture No 6 **Marijke Heuff**; private garden
Picture No 7 **Marijke Heuff**; private garden
Picture No 8 **The Garden Picture Library/Gary Rogers**; private garden, Little Thakeham
Picture No 9 **The Garden Picture Library/Ron Sutherland**; private garden, Fairman
Picture No 10 **Hugh Palmer**; Villandry, France
Picture No 11 **Marijke Heuff**; The Coach House, Little Haseley, Oxfordshire
Picture No 12 **The Garden Picture Library/Jerry Pavia**; Deepwood Sales, Oregon, USA
Picture No 13 **The Garden Picture Library/Gary Rogers**; private garden
Picture No 14 **Georges Lévêque**; Mary Rumary (garden architect), Westley Waterless, Suffolk
Picture No 15 **The Garden Picture Library/Ron Sutherland**; Michael Balston (designer)
Picture No 16 **The Garden Picture Library/Ron Sutherland**; Duane Paul Design Team

63